ial. Clarke

SUZUKI
BASS SCHOOL

Volume 3
Bass Part
Revised Edition

CONTENTS

		Page	Track Numbers*
1	Moon Over the Ruined Castle, *R. Taki*	3	1
2	Minuet No. 2, *J. S. Bach*	4	2
3	Ode to Joy, *L. van Beethoven*	6	3
4	Andantino (Enjoyable Morning), *S. Suzuki*	7	4
	Tonalization E♭ Major Scale	7	5
5	Trilling Waltz, *V. Dixon*	8	6
6	Sweet Georgia Brown, *B. Bernie, M. Pinkard and K. Casey, arr. D. Swaim*	11	7
7	Largo From the "New World Symphony," *A. Dvořák*	12	8
8	Bourrée, *G. F. Handel*	13	9
9	Gavotte, *F. J. Gossec*	14	10
10	So What, *M. Davis, arr. D. Swain*	17	11
11	A Gaelic Melody, *C. Minkler*	18	12
12	L'Elephant, *C. Saint-Saëns*	20	13
13	Scherzo, *C. Webster*	22	14

AMPV: 1.00

© 2014, 2004, 1996 Dr. Shinichi Suzuki
Sole publisher for the entire world except Japan:
Summy-Birchard, Inc.
Exclusive print rights administered by Alfred Music
All rights reserved. Printed in USA.

Available in the following formats: Book (0376S), Book & CD Kit (40733), CD (0380)

Book
ISBN-10: 0-87487-376-2
ISBN-13: 978-0-87487-376-4

Book & CD Kit
ISBN-10: 0-7390-9715-6
ISBN-13: 978-0-7390-9715-1

The Suzuki name, logo and wheel device
are trademarks of Dr. Shinichi Suzuki
used under exclusive license by Summy-Birchard, Inc.

Any duplication, adaptation or arrangement of the compositions
contained in this collection requires the written consent of the Publisher.
No part of this book may be photocopied or reproduced in any way without permission.
Unauthorized uses are an infringement of the U.S. Copyright Act and are punishable by law.

INTRODUCTION

FOR THE STUDENT: This material is part of the worldwide Suzuki Method® of teaching. The companion recording should be used along with this publication. A piano accompaniment book is also available for this material.

FOR THE TEACHER: In order to be an effective Suzuki teacher, ongoing education is encouraged. Each regional Suzuki association provides teacher development for its membership via conferences, institutes, short-term and long-term programs. In order to remain current, you are encouraged to become a member of your regional Suzuki association, and if not already included, the International Suzuki Association.

FOR THE PARENT: Credentials are essential for any teacher you choose. We recommend you ask your teacher for his or her credentials, especially those relating to training in the Suzuki Method®. The Suzuki Method® experience should foster a positive relationship among the teacher, parent and child. Choosing the right teacher is of the utmost importance.

To obtain more information about the Suzuki Association in your region, please contact:

International Suzuki Association
www.internationalsuzuki.org

1
Moon Over the Ruined Castle

Rentaro Taki

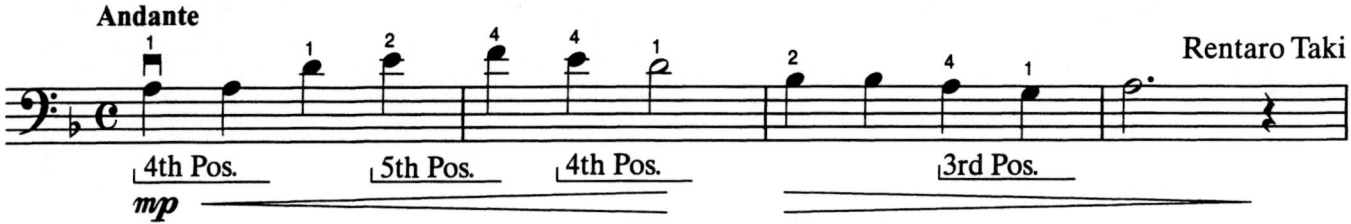

Shifting Preparation

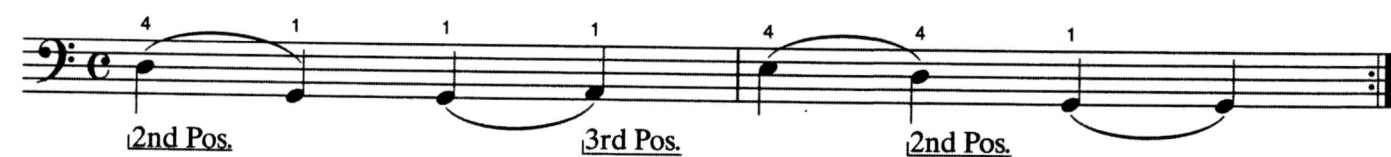

2
Minuet No. 2

J.S. Bach

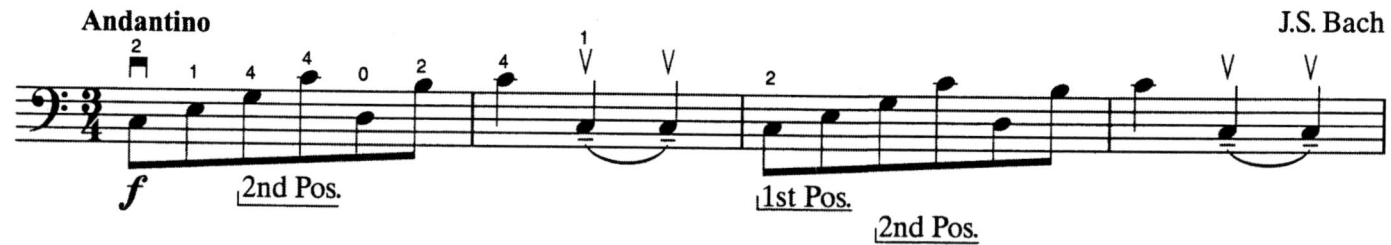

2nd Pos.
1st Pos.
2nd Pos.
1st Pos.
3rd Pos.
1/2 Pos.
2nd Pos.
1st Pos.
dim.
2nd Pos.
3rd Pos.
2nd Pos.
1st Pos.

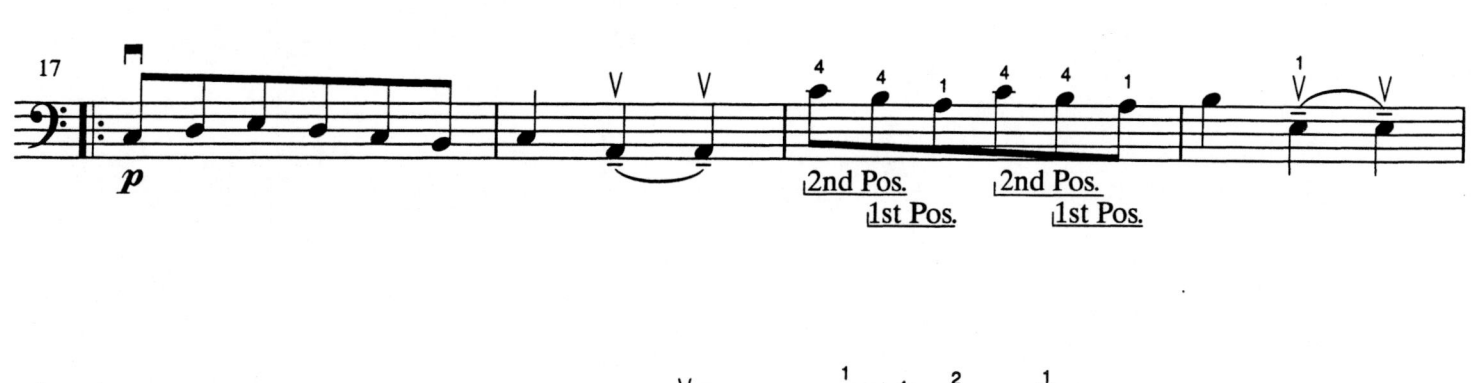

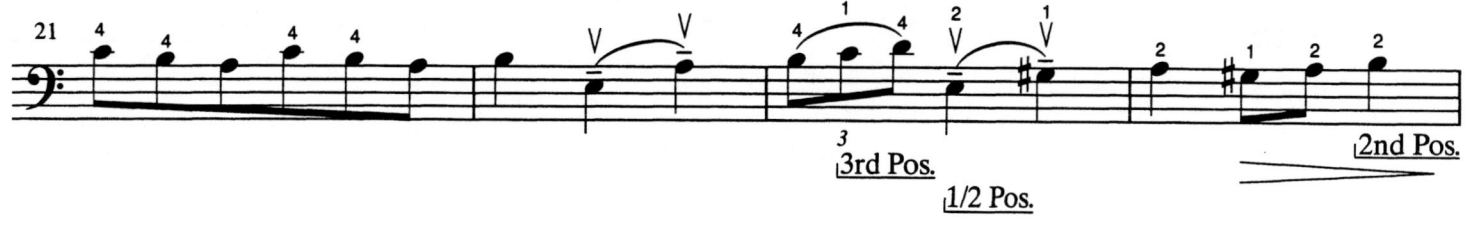

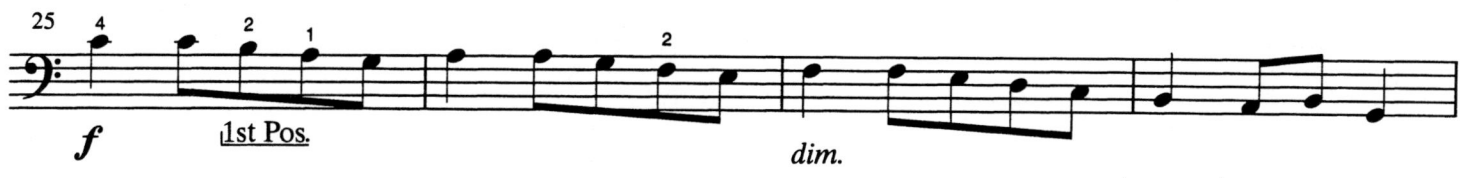

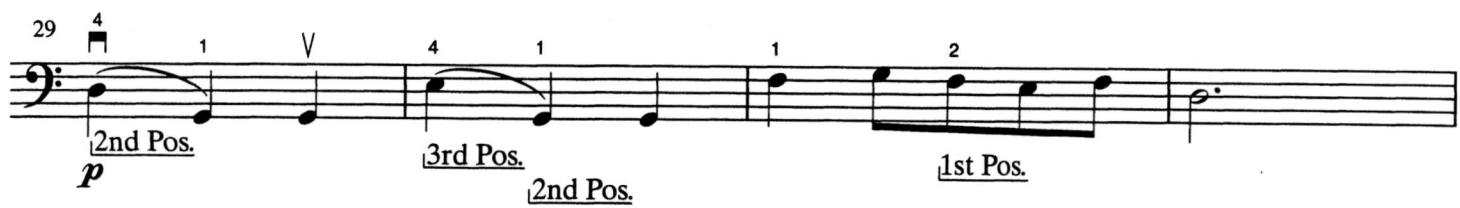

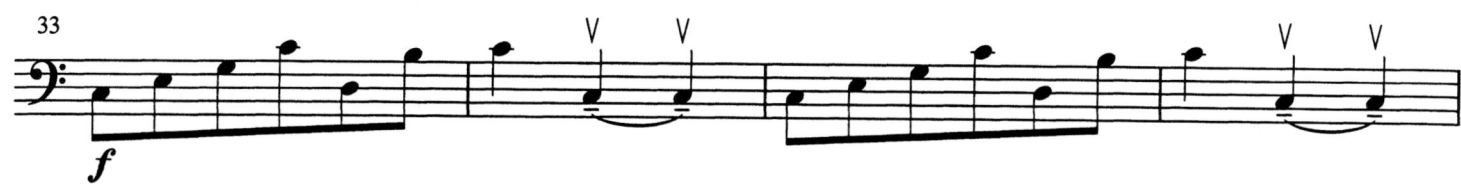

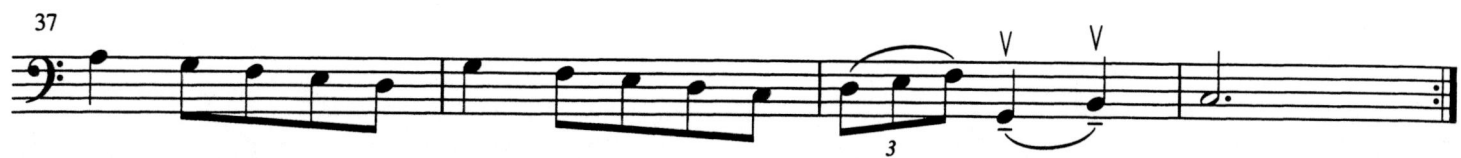

Preparatory Exercises for Thumb Position

Ode to Joy
from Symphony No. 9

L. van Beethoven

Andantino
(Enjoyable Morning)

S. Suzuki

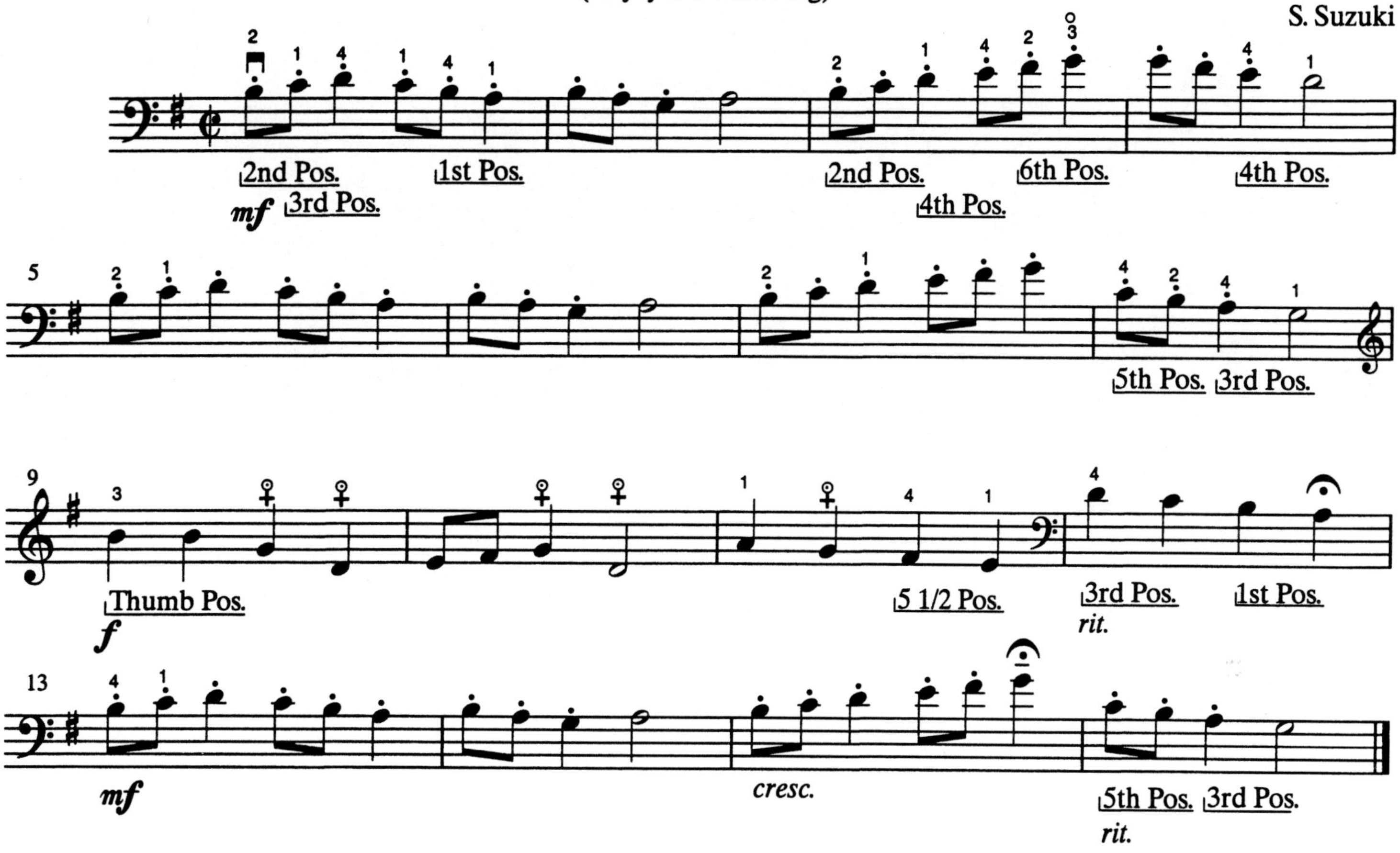

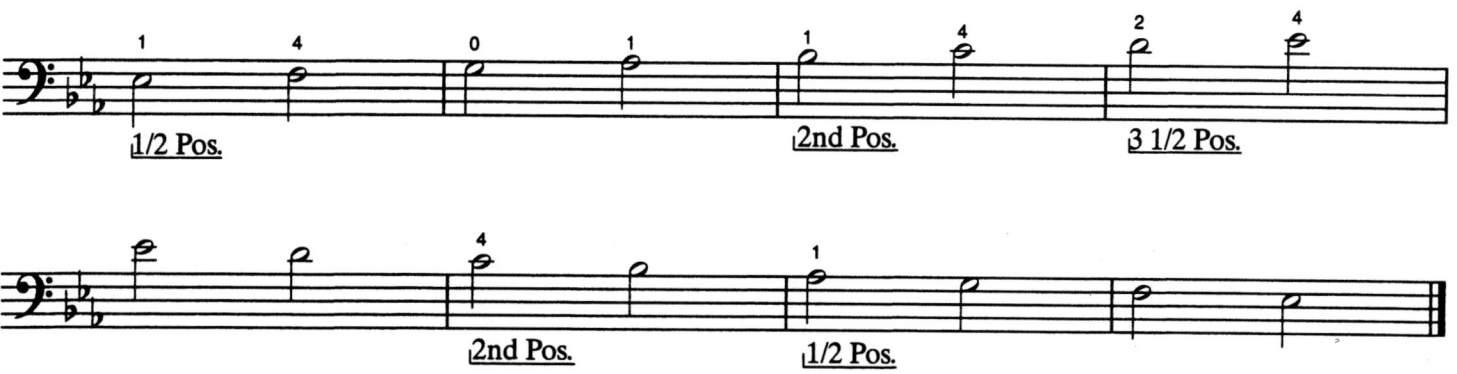

Tonalization
E♭ Major Scale

5

Trilling Waltz

Tempo di valse

Virginia Dixon

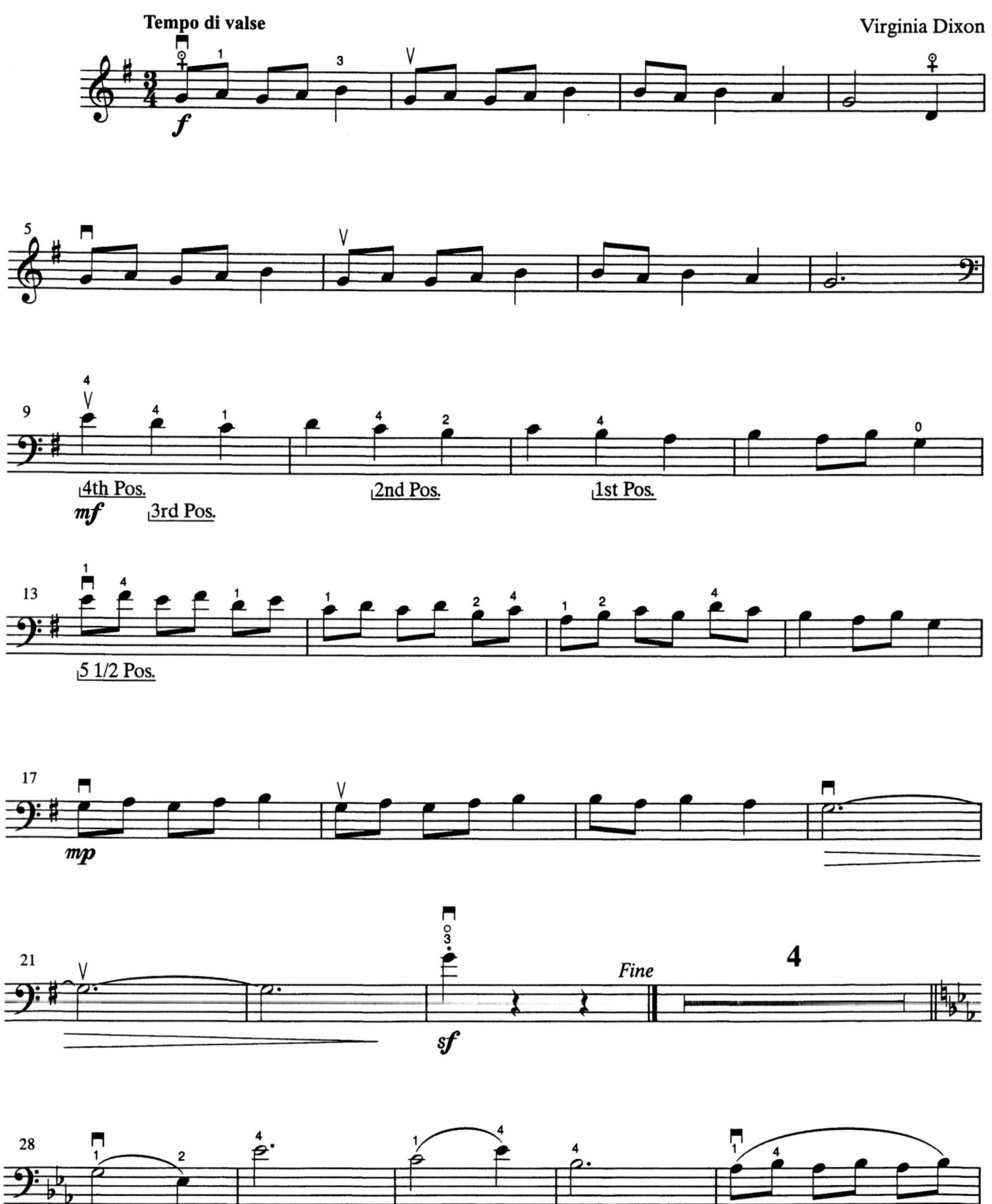

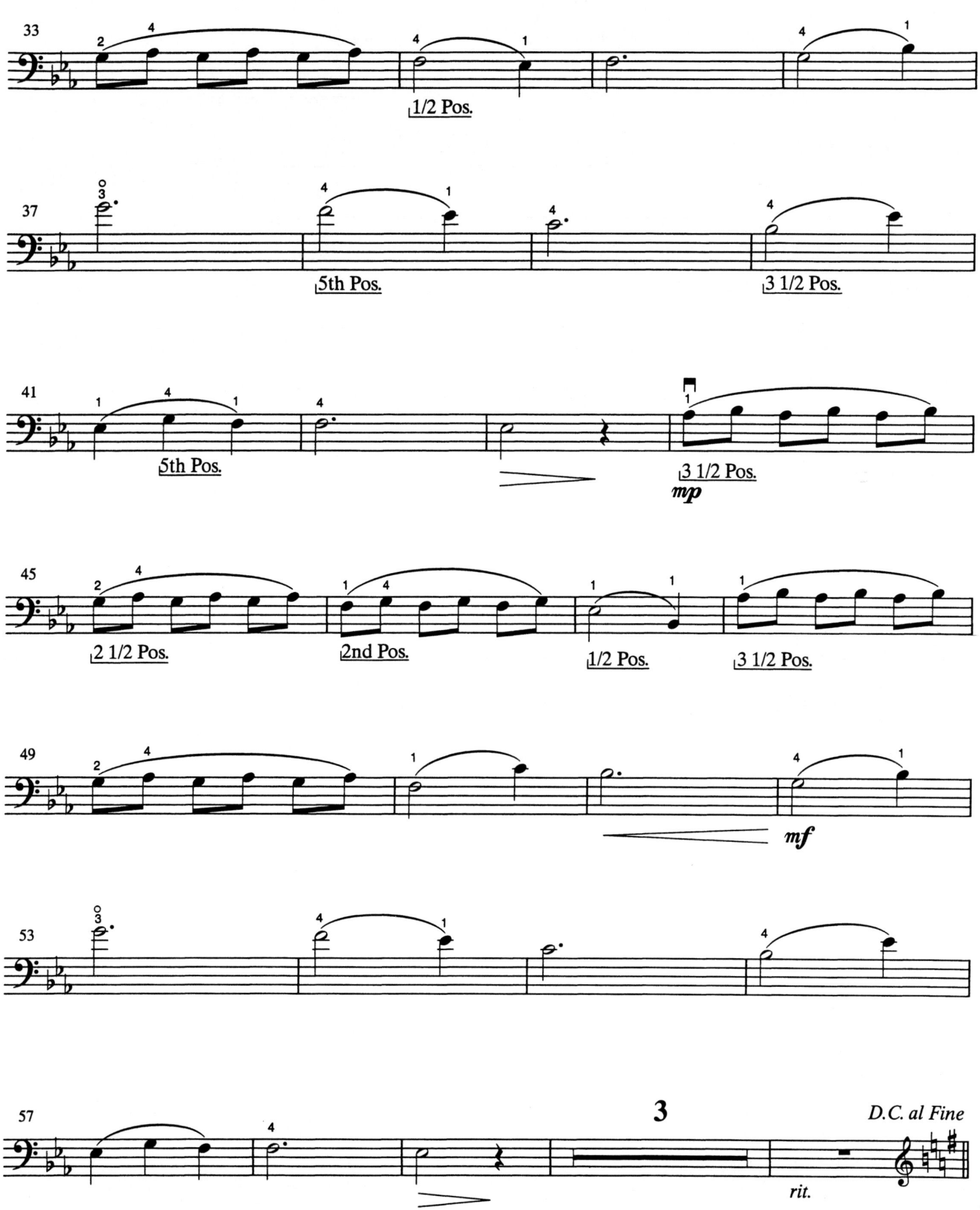

Preparation for Sweet Georgia Brown

11

6
Sweet Georgia Brown

**Words and Music by
Ben Bernie, Maceo Pinkard and
Kenneth Casey
Arranged by Daniel Swaim**

*Bar and lift the fourth finger after playing pizzicato. Play pizzicato with the right thumb at the lower end of the fingerboard for this double-stop chord.

© 1925 WARNER BROS. INC. (Renewed)
This Arrangement © 1996 WARNER BROS. INC.
All Rights Reserved

7
Largo from the "New World Symphony"

A. Dvořák

8. Bourree

G.F. Handel

This page has been left blank intentionally to facilitate page turns.

Preparatory Exercises for So What

11
A Gaelic Melody

Chester Minkler

Preparatory Exercise for L' Elephant

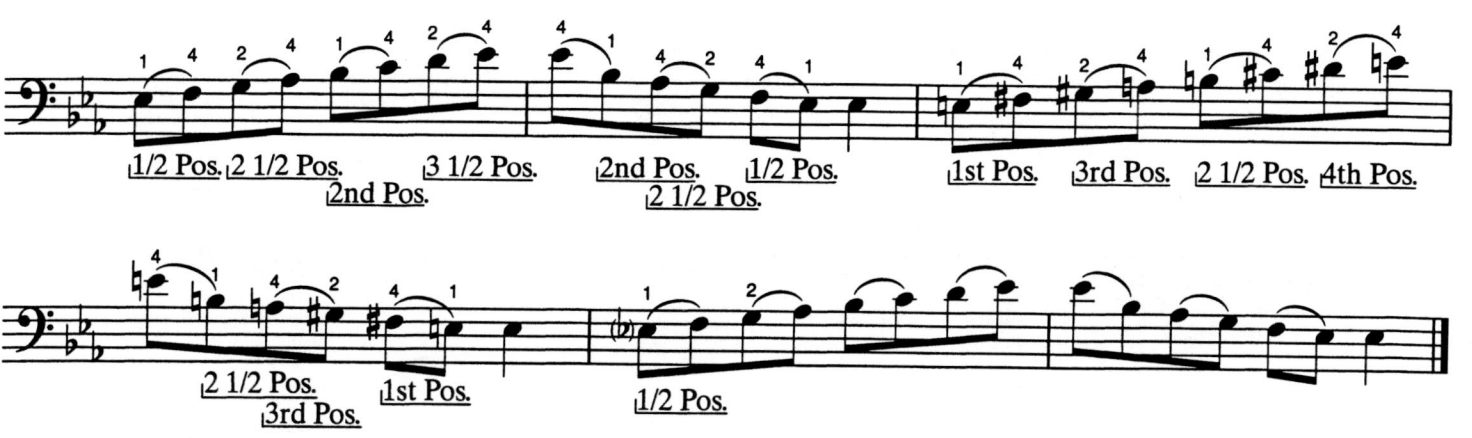

Preparation for Scherzo

13
Scherzo